LETTERS FROM EARTH:

THE ENVIRONMENT SPEAKS

STORY-PLAYS AND POEMS FROM THE PROGRESSIVE SIDE

This volume was written as an internet-based project, working collaboratively with hundreds of individuals who submitted important events in their lives and these were transformed into stories and poems by the author. They are not in a special order and rather, reflect the flow of conversations as they occurred.

Lonnie Hicks
March 2009

The Earth Speaks

I am the Earth,
your mother:

and you are my children.

I am from the dust
of a thousand, billion, trillion stars

careened in the milky way
accreting from millions
of scarring asteroid hits
and comet cataclysms.

Hot lava poured across my face,
volcanic steam
seethed through my pores
and I was Rocky World
with an Iron Core.

For eons I endured
more scars, more collusions
yet from all of this
I grew life,
blue oceans
and amino acids
from which
I fashioned

the first cell
come alive;

and then colonies of cells
into more complex cells
then whole beings;
you.

I nurtured the small creatures,
your brothers and sisters.

I gave you the moon
for silver nights,

the stars for inspiration
a magnetic shield
to protect your from the sun's burning rays;

I gave you food, animals and trees
so that you might thrive.

You are all my children
whom I have reared in paradise;
in a world of plenty
shielded from the void.

I took you from the caves
and showed you fire
sacrificed my own wood trees
so that you might cook your food;
gave you animal skins
of my own creation
to shelter you from winter.

Gave you water.

I showed you the beauty of the stars.
but alas too,
a brain big enough to study war.

And you did discover war;
you discovered hate;

you took my abundance
and made of it destruction.

My forests now burn
ignited by your hand;

you have rent my face with mining scars
quarry scabs;
polluted my oceans and rivers
for beads and baubles;
and fleeting shiny things

and then you threw this garbage away;
whole pollution mountains now
tower over my terrain..

There seems no retreat from you
and the relentlessness
with which you pursue
all this
for reasons
I do not fathom
and it wearies me;
frightens me.

Hear me my children;
my fate is now entrapped
with yours:
whether you live
is whether I live,

what you do
can destroy my oceans ;

I would return to being a cold rocky world
in the crushing dark;
my blues
will grey
and blacken.

Hear me my children
for we are family.

I Am the Aquifer

I am the Aquifer
in the deep gorge.

I'm rain.

I was water for the many herds
that drank from me.
I'm shelter from the deluge;
treasure house of oxygen
and minerals
which seep
into my rooms
in deep soils replenishing.

I'm life's ecology.
The water-bag
of chemistry
and you are my children.

Hear my sad tears.

I taste dirty waterings
and poisonings.

Plentiful I was in the
early years,
under deserts I was salvation for the caravans,
well source for the Egyptians
reservoir for villagers,
beast bird and fowl;
insect and amoebae
all drank from me.
I was the culture source for all life.
My rivers spawned civilization.

Now, I am retreated.
A mixed drink,
consumed

with a steel straw,
nonrenewable;
sipped with too much
over-confidence
and greed.

My table is thin.
My offerings slim.
My purity waned.

I seep below my own level
scattering precious tear-drops
vulcanized to bloody steam
and sometimes I explode
up up
to the blasting cone
and I am deposited amid the ruin,
into the gorge again.

I am slower;
my cycle recedes,
my dry tears howl.

I see Harmony's Crown
crashing down.

I see the End of Plenty
and Horsemen moving
looming, looming, looming;
climate backing up,
bent down eyes,
reeling waterfalls
receding times,
calm resignations,

generations lined up,
against the wall,

whole cities caterwaul,
lakes pirouette,
swirling times sweep up,
all regrets,
all maybes,

all lost,
all gone.

I was the Aquifer
life sustaining;
now, a shadowy voice
dumbfounded
drilled down
in weeping earth.

Smart Apes

The trees are leaving;
lurched away;
heading magnetic north;
sap cooled
and cold.

The elms,
uproot themselves;
and go.

Shade is gone.
The house is warm less;
night prolonged.

I see birds laboring west
unclear and direction-less.

Nature's abandonment
is profound.

I see no humming bird
at the outside feeder
now for weeks.
A tragedy.

Sorrow is a hoof-less stag,
the stunted bud on the flowerless tree,
the wind that weeps.

The bad air is Grey Green

'Beware of Smart Apes
wielding intelligence
uncontrolled.'

Hope is the mutancy
which may overcome Smart Ape Tendencies;
how likely
how unlikely
much depends

**upon the answer
to the query.**

Robin Suicide

A robin committed suicide today
flew right into my living room window
it's chilly mid-November;
maybe he was heading south.

Blam! The sound, and wings blurred;
he went straight to the ground.

No way could he have missed the house,
it's large, the window is below the roof,
he was not flying with other birds,
or forgot to look.

Like a jet with not a single flap down,
he hit the window full-throttle.

I got up and took a look
expecting him to stir and fly
but he didn't move below; lying quiet.

I went down to see.
Yes a Robin, older, red breast.
didn't stir, didn't move.
I touched him.
Neck awry.
Probably broken.
Instant Death.

What to do?
I looked around for mourners.
There were none.

This Robin was solo,
all on his own.

It didn't seem fitting
to conduct a garbage can burial,
so I said a few words, cursed,
and decided to bury him in dirt.

It was easy.

Picked him up by his tail
took him to the back yard;
had some compost there.
Dug a shallow grave, mumbled something;
lay him in there;
patted the top; my good deed done.

A dead robin in my yard, flying south
by my window dead; undone.
But, I am thinking maybe he did it deliberately.

There were some clues.
How can a Robin miss
a great big house,
hit the pane, drop dead down,
there must be some explanation
some hidden clue I'd missed.

Maybe he was an old Robin, diseased,
disoriented by Alzheimer's, or a bird pestilence,
chemicals or what.
Could have been a bird fight of some kind:
he was fleeing, running away in defeat.
The Crows around here are criminals and tough;
the Robin could have lost in a West Side Story Bird Fight.

I decided to go outside and look up to see for myself;
look for clues to the Robins' death
not content for the time being
to dismiss it lightly
as dumb bird lost.

So... from Robin's height my window pane looks straight
on through the house, out through the back windows and
on into the yard trees.

Ah ha; the Robin's keen eyes
could have been looking at
my backyard trees,
flying straight and hard, not seeing
the first window pane. Blam and there you are-
an explanation which made some sense

but having there, too,
a painful irony within.

His grave lay beneath those trees
he was so intent
to reach.
Dead Robin flying fast,
gaze fixed upon his own death.
How Shakespearean.

I think final destinations,
as in where we will die:
inside hospitals, on the road,
in a plane for most of us
is unknown.
My robin could see his own demise;
the means to him were clear and unclear;
my window, both opaque
and transparent.

Ah, again how Shakespearian.
A Robin causality;

wonder if he had kids.

A Homo Sapien

We are the Smart Apes
who rose from the African Plains
who learned to eat meat
and grow large brains;

I see Cro-Magnon man
and Neanderthal man;
living in the Cave
fashioning spear tips;

I Cro-Magnon Man
came from the Middle East
to Europe
to find there Neanderthal,
short,
stocky
slow.

I could see
he had no knowledge of serrated
spear tips:

was no match
for my nimble technologies.
and the warming climate.

I inter-married and /or dispersed him
until today I am all that is left.

I brought fire to Neanderthal;
in it simmers his remains.

I see other animals
learning fear
as the Ape spread
from Africa
to Java, to Asia
and Europe;

There were halting migrations
twice made
driven by climate change;

the whole human race
dwindled down to 14 thousand individuals;
a tiny gene pool
the ancestors of our entire progeny.

We are all mutants
from a gene pool too small;
We are genetic experiments;
incomplete
paradoxical
killers and despoilers
peace lovers;
creators
and destroyers;
an animal with
a bad genetic start.

I see the development of the opposable thumb;
tooling making
art, technology, the family
war and genocide
Religiosity
and non-religiosity
all in the mix.

There was tyranny,
democracy,
fascism, capitalism
socialism, communism
all from the same brain.

Here comes History,
generational knowledge;
books;
computers.

We Apes touch other worlds.
Send our voices into space
grasp the nature of the universe

invented the concept of Love
threaten the planet with permanent
change
pollute our own nest
invent science
enslave millions
and pave under the trees.

We are Homo Sapiens
self named 'Wise Men'
And we live in this Irony.

Flushed

In my garden gambol
green beetles
by twos and threes,

who sing to High Tulips
blushing pink
in harmonies.

Flushed,
adoration-framed,
they rainbow through
emotions gained
from beetle songs
choir sung.

I part the foliage clef
to observe what enchantment deft
musical beetles pant
to flowered plants
swaying in the green.

I am transfixed
in this gloaming,

where songs stroke
the airy night;

uplifting
tulip bulbs-
rhapsodized
and honey dewed.

On me then
euphonies:

Beatles sing
because we don't,
to balm absence's pain.
They sing our song
of high praise;
because we won't,

for tulips,
gardens, soil and loam.

We are the children
who've lost
the songs
which were mother's songs
now vague;
distant,
gone.

Our ears
deaf now,
withdrawn.

The beetles stand in for us
sing our songs
in their metallic
greens,

arpeggios falling to
my journal page
explaining
why they sing

to tulip bulbs,
flushed
on the green:

all quiet now-
each bulb
reminded-
they are loved.

In Between

I walked through Heaven's Gates
and St. Peter did not recognize me;

I had not sinned enough to warrant
detection.

I walked through checkpoint after checkpoint
unseen
bathed in light
but opaque
more presence than me,
consumed with curiosity about what lay beyond;
beyond Heavens Gate.

There were lights and sprites, visions and presences
protuberances and quivering entities
all there and not there
around me
but none spoke to me.

Is God's domain heavenly
or a way-point to Limbo,
Hell's Vestibule
or Sacred Angel Space?

The light weakened my eyes
until I could only hear voices
but could not see;

I groped lost,
listening,
hearing
until
I felt the force of transport,

and suddenly
I was hovering above
an edifice
being floated inside
where I materialized
before a still brighter light

which contained the face of
what I thought must be God.

It was too much for me,
my mind blanked
I could not think
beyond a steady rising euphoria;
bodiless
and ether-like
I rose on a soft breeze
quivering in my soul
gradually landing
back on my bed;
my body
remembering
he who touched me
without touching me
who moved his hand
over me
returned my heart to me.

And now,
I lay prone
shaking
feeling the weight of me
on the bed
discharged from the dream;
abandoned
to reality
Not ready for heaven,
not sinful enough for Hell;

still here on earth
unreconciled,
to the In-Between.

Progress?

There was this struggling;
a knife-sharp shovel blade
dug deep in Earth's rib-cage.

tall tree limbs severed
which drop to the ground;
habitat homes invaded
and brook arteries polluted;
by drugs and poisons.

The warming eye of sun-
blinded by carbon rain
stinging neon gas
make sun-sets
and sun downs
red red red.

The animals
flee
to hovels
beneath
the shrinking ground
and pavements slather
on more and more concrete.

Mountains recede;
worn down;
the ocean waters
rise lapping the scars
to take back the
crowded shores.

Smoke stacks
and coal pits;
Nuclear plants
and nuclear fission.

At all this
the Earth sheds
a near final tear,
weeping

**asking:
is this
Progress?**

Fairy Stars

My uncle Dan
was a Harlem Man
danced extra light on his feet
smiles like radiant sun
talked up close to ya
comfortable with himself
and you could always
smell his cologne.

The ladies loved him;
loved that laugh of his
he always had flattery for them
often given.

Uptown.
down town
he never came to the house
what without a gift;
loved us 'chilings'
soft candy
and wild stories
which always had a point.

'Time was' he'd say'
'that there was a meadow
over that way
till they paved it over'

'Your grandmother-
why she came from 500 acres
in the deep south-
til they taxed her family out.

Had to leave the land;
she still bitter
and put out.

We all
here
in this family
immigrants

and runaways
most free,
some slaves.

'Now'
he'd say
'don't trade
plantation slave
for city slave
get your own business.
Be an 'enter-pre-newr'

Knew the stars
and summer nights'
would have us all look up:

'Now see that fairy princess there
right there between those five stars
that's God looking over all little girls
and those stars are God's fairy saints.

If ever you need
just look up
and they'll be there watching there;
ready to take care of you.

Each night
go to the window
be sure to say goodnight to 'em'

He died in my sophomore year.

I traveled to Chicago to say goodbye.

He had asked all the women he loved
to leave a white rose on his casket.
And white roses were there

everywhere, everywhere
as far as the eye could see
and that included a long-stemmed white rose
from me;

lovingly placed;

remembering
those fairy saints;
and Uncle Dan
looking up
all bright-eyed
saying;
'Now say goodnight;
they can hear you.

I believe to this day
he was right.

A Wind Breeze

I am the Southern Breeze;
bearer of the Wisteria;

The North Wind
from where the ice blows.

I am the Lover's Caress
on sandy beach,

The Wind-Mill Corn Grinder
and the Water Wheel;

I am invisible
yet everywhere
I blow all over
this globe.
.
I've billowed your sails
propelled your ships
carried you
to far lands;
opened to you
new worlds.

True, too,
I have blown your houses down
tornadoed the things you love.

I am too
the wind of Bad Luck
and Ill Fate.

I am the wind in your lungs.

I carry the oxygen you breathe
first life's halting blush
and likely the last to leave
your body's chest
and you expire.

Now my clear air

is grey

smoky
smoke-stacked
and my once proud life
on this planet
is near extinct.

Sixty miles;
just an hour's drive
of me and my oxygen
are your only shield;
against the void of outer space;
its cosmic rays,
the deadly magnetic fields
meteors and asteroids
all would crash down
were it not for me;

the sun's infrared rays
would burn if I did not block.
and provide to you
a cloak.

Indeed,
I am the life you breathe
from birth's first
to death's last.

You've felt me
on your face
riding the plains,
or walking the meadows;

I am
the Invisible Sea
you sail
and your final
Destiny.
I am the wind;
your oxygen.

Angels and Birds

Angels and birds fly
altitude I guess
provides perspective
from heights where
we see
the Earth is just a blue ball
rotating in space,
with millions below
unaware of the
Dark Surround;
of Moons and Galaxies.

.

If we listen
we hear
happiness,
anger,
and bliss
all in the cacophonous mix,
and it then seems
that Angel eyes and ears
see true perspective;
birds then
must be
our earthly angels on the wing.

They go south
and come North
too
having seen
much along the way;
they, too,
are lofted
by wings
and they are the closest
I guess
I will get
to heavenly things.

Here's to the Eagle
and the Sparrow
the Chickadee

the Cardinal
and the Crow
for they all soar
high
close to the Angels
and closer than we
to Heaven.

An Icicle Kiss

I am the Winter Flower
she said
the opposite of the Summer Ones.

My blooms
peak in deep snow
and I weather
hail, sleet and angry gale.

My Summer Kin
know the Sun.

I live beneath
White Winter's Glow
withstanding
blizzard wind
as furies blow.

I produce
anti-cold;
survive
winter's
frozen mold.

My petals
are steel-forged
for winter has made
me strong.

My bulb forces its way
up through frozen ground
and defiant
I face worst Winter's onslaughts.

My petals
fold and unfold
peak,
and stare Winter down.
I am the Winter Flower
beautiful in my Ice Tower.

I too,
have my Ice Prince
who plants upon me
an Icicle Kiss
beneath diamond shining
beautiful,
frosty
Wintry Stars.

The Shark and I

We humans evolved 100,000 years ago
from just 4 amino acids
forming our DNA
but note the Shark has been here 100 million years.

And genetically,
we and Sharks are 95% the same.

So who owns this planet?

A Wounded Angel

How sad to see
thousands of butterfly wings
freshly plucked
scattered on the ground.

How sad to see
Wounded Angels flounder
at the cliffs edge
one by one
falling into the abyss,

a young girl holding
out her hand
trying to hold her sandy heart
pieces
from sifting through her fingers
grain by grain
blown away by the wind,

Orphan Eyes
slowly closing-
taken by the Caped One.

How sad to see The Haunted of the World
closing the door to Hope,

Rainbow pieces
scattered along
the freeways.

All these sad scenes-
blazing memories-
motivate us
to say
never again to:

ripped up butterfly wings;
wounded angels floundering
atomized sandy young girl hearts;
 dead children,
Hope murdered in the streets

Rainbows crying sadly
along side our freeways.
All too sad.

All too much
to ever forget.

All the more necessary to prevent.

Humans should not tolerate this,
we
mustn't.

Jobism-According to Uncle Bob

'Jobism'
he said
'the real disease of the 2Oth century'
Bob was warming up to the topic.

'Now you take my grandfather,
what he wanted was his own piece of land
the ability to run his own life
he didn't work all his life for a job.
He worked for land and the independence
that land meant.

It has been that way for all of history of the human race.

From the cave man marking up the cave walls
to the rancher, the farmer
and the homesteader,
all we have ever wanted was a piece of land
to call our own.

My people came here not for a job
but for freedom.
Now we are settling for cubicles.

Mere one-hundred years ago
they taxed us off the land
gave to the corporations;
the farmers left the land,
got herded
into the dirty cities
plopped down into factories
becoming wage-slaves.

My Granddad is still bitter to this dad.

Now our kids are taught be good,
get a good education
and try to get a good wage-slave job.

One hundred years ago
it was get your own piece of land,

be independent,
don't be beholden to any man,

don't let the authorities run your life.
What a change huh?

This has had for more impact
than we think.
Hitler's minions asked why did they gas the Jews
and their answers were, 'it was my job.'

People in experiments will kill other people
if scientists in white lab coats tell them it's ok to do so.

Whole nations go to war and maim
because somebody told them it was their job to do so.

Job one
means obedience is number two,
obedience to those that you might not ever obey
except for they tell you
obey me or your family starves.
or you can't get a good job.

We need to sever the wage-slave
from the job
which enslaves.

Cities never really worked
they create wealth for the few
and poverty for the many. Still does.

Why let 20 social agencies surround
single moms living there and expect
that to work?

My idea, ' he said'
is I don't want no job
I want independence.

Then he smiled.

Rainbow Walking

If I walk to the end of my rainbow
will there be a pot of gold?

Will rainbow travel be worth
the hassle?

If I succeed
then suppose
I find that I am not as worthy
as other Rainbow Walkers?

If I am not
I'll be exposed
as fraudulent.

If I walk to the end of my rainbow
while I be happy?
Or just as sad
as I now am?

How do I know that Rainbow Walking
is worth it all?

My uncle used to say
that 'having dreams that you
or the world will be different at the
end of the rainbow
has a flaw.

After walking and succeeding
you'll still be there.

Rainbows don't glow
if you don't.'

Never understood
what he was talking about
till later on.

Now I really really like
the Rainbow in me

and no matter where I walk
its aways there
and I realize
I am
my own
pot of gold.

Twilight's Love

I am summer's breath
light as the sky
floaty as a feather tip.

I love warmth
and humming bird flutterings
which
to me smell
summer sweet.

You are intense,
a darker hue
almost possessed
almost obsessed
with wanting to spend
every minute with me.

Yet
can Summer Fire
and Winter Cold
cohabitate?

Can my Fire
melt your Ice?

Can your intensity
bend my summer
to gravity?

I say lets take away
our layered clothes
and go bath
in the ocean.

You say
someone might see.

I say dance here
on leafy ground
and you worry
out loud
about
being
too
demonstrative.

But if there is
attraction at all
it is in possession-ness
and you have plenty of that;
part of me
responds
to being
possessed.
I like it.

It offsets
my summer levity;
seems a balance
to
too much Summer Light.

And after all
isn't romance
the color of twilight
and candles
in that in-between light
not winter, nor summer-hued?

You're obsessed with me
and I walk you to the Cave's Mouth
and show you light
which in the instant's moment
exposes you to
the Summer Side.

Isn't this then
more than mutual balancing?

Thirty years
now
we have
called
it
Love.

It's still working.

All Power

If I could take the world
into my world;
If I could be God-like
what would I do
with my All-Power?

Would I make Peace
World-Wide?
What of Poverty?
What of our environment?

I could gather all riches
to my self,
make my friends powerful or rich
or both;
help my parents?

Ask for more Power?
Use my Power to
make more Power?

What would I do with
All Power to do Anything?

Would I ask for Love?
Force someone to Love
me too?

I don't like All-Power
as I think about it.

What would I choose?

Could I have a few powers?
One or two?
All at the same time?

But even so
I would be
the only one.
and maybe lonely?

But if I could
and the price is lonely
why wouldn't I?
.
To have that power
would get me back
now
where I am now
lonely.

What good then
All-Power?

This will take
some thinking
out.

Circles

The Circling Through;
the Sun;
The Returning Cycle;
the Completion;
Infinity;
The Eye.

All these
are symbolized
by a line
which
circles
back to its own beginning.

The Community Closes Ranks
and Closes Off;
The Encirclement
The Focused Effort.

The Linking of These.

the First Cell.

We're All
Circles

and
though this comprehend
endless connectedness
and the sense
of beginnings & endings
we exist within.

Force Majeure

How then does Force Majeure
threaten all existence;
often wielded by the bluntest instrument?

How can it be
that rank murder
can Imagination extinguish?

How can human genius be crushed
by a louts blow,
ignorant of kindness
or the million years it took
to create the opposable thumb
then used to bludgeon the human skull.

What justice is there then
in a world so arduously created
but so easily destroyed
by means foul and low?

Why does Nature provide
for evolution's progress
yet not allow it to survive,

but instead subject us to the lows
and highs
of periodic extinguishments,
of starting over and over again

with new blueprints
for new flora and fauna,
which after millennia
can be dashed by a another rock
incoming from outer space?

Where is the plan here?
Where is the justice scale
which makes this make sense?

If we then succumb to flaming craters
or rampant disease
if all Genius can be murdered
on the dark streets,
What wherefore is the point here?

Such gloom and toil
aways there
looms over every tree
and every unsuspecting fleur de lis.

Nature herself cannot be the blame
for nature too blows up in fiery steam.

Where then is the locus true;
the Explanation Grandiloquent
which fixes the true locus of blame?

Is all Cold Physics;
random luck
and ugly death in
future states?

Does honor lay
in resisting this fate;
to struggle against the
the Extinguishment Date?

Too weighty here
for me to see.

I lay me down
Headache Bound
to contemplate
this another day
but understanding
thus;
that the end is never the end
but only the pause
before the new blueprint

and the story
renews.

Our burden is renewal;
death gives way to the new
but,
then again
all that sounds
very familiar too.

The Muse- Whither America?

I asked the Muse Whither America?

'I see millions in the broken cities
crowding debt,
unhappiness.

I see family's un-affordable,
single parents struggling;
.

I see the children no longer able to afford the big houses
and the old ones abandon the homestead,
and crowd back to the cities.

The young ones can't find work
its five to a house.
.

The Americans, the British, the Italians
the Russians, all of Western Europe
can not
duplicate themselves and they perish
replaced by the poor ones from the South
and the East.

All the world comes together to confront Destiny.
Whither the Planet?

But hope there is:
There will be in America
repatriation of the rural lands;
the abandonment of the cites
and massive building of rural technology-based enclaves;
smart technology driven, green based and self sufficient.

America's salvation there.

Economies will move toward barter exchange
because currency will fail,
replaced by new systems and gains in efficiency

Government will devolve to less control
less bureaucracy;
more local control
weak confederations instead.

The village life returns.

Crafts replace portions of profit-based technology.

Old skills of self-sufficiency revive.

Nation states are weakened,
and cross national enclaves emerge
where ideas cross boundaries.

Real democracy will thrive in smaller settings.

This will be
whether there is disaster
or planning for this.

Disaster will give us small enclaves
but bands of marauders
and bandit bands
who leave the cites
when the five day supply of food gives out;
their enclaves are forced and violent.

The better way is the one I describe.

In your life-time son
40 years hence
this will be
but which future.
will it be?